MW01515869

Dogs... *Made Easy!*

A New Owner's Manual

to Otto –
Good luck w/ your people training!
Kathie Compton

by Kathie Compton

⋙⋘

Fly 'n Dog Studio

Dogs... *Made Easy!*
A New Owner's Manual

By Kathie Compton © 2006

Printed and bound in the United States of America

ISBN 0-9786557-0-2

Published by: Fly 'n Dog Studio
P.O. Box 516
Marfa, TX 79843
Phone: 432-729-4292
Fax: 432-729-4290
E-mail: flyndog@texasdogtrainer.com

To order this book visit: www.texasdogtrainer.com
or call: 1-800-667-9464

＞＜

This book is dedicated to my parents for giving me the "dog gene", to my friends Susan Thompson and Jack for starting me on the training path, and to all the animals I have known for putting up with me while I was learning, as well as to those who continue to teach me.

Special thanks go to Burt Compton, Sierra Trees, Jennifer Rodriguez, Alexis Latner, Lynn Hoover, Betty Mueller, and the photographers for their advice, assistance and contributions.

Gratitude goes to my best friend Cozy for her patience with me while I ignored her to write this book.

＞＜

— The Dog Models —

Argyle, *a Miniature Dachshund owned by Michelle Kirk...*
Bonnie, *a Boxer owned by Joni Marginot...*
Calvin, *a Boxer owned by Joni Marginot...*
Cooper, *an American Bull Dog Mix owned by Karen Kirkpatrick...*
Cozy Dog, *a Yorkshire Terrier owned by the Author, Kathie Compton...*

Eleusis, *an American Pit Bull Terrier owned by Kathleen Bell...*
Jasmine, *a Rottweiler owned by Robin Grubbs...*
Theo, *a Beagle Mix (at "Rainbow Bridge") owned by Anastacia Singleton...*
Wesley, *a Black Labrador Retriever owned by Anastacia Singleton...*
Zada and Azrael, *Yorkshire Terriers owned by Donna Husnik...*

— Table of Contents —

— Introduction —

Dogs... *Made Easy!* *A New Owner's Manual* was written to help new dog owners understand their dogs. Whether you are training alone or with an instructor, this book will help you get the most out of your effort.

Each chapter represents the most common difficulties dog owners face. It is not a how-to manual for teaching specific commands such as "Sit", "Come" or "Stay", although some suggestions for these commands are included. Written in a concise, easy-to-read format, this book will give you a basic understanding of dog "psychology" and how you can maintain control over your dog's behavior, train new behaviors, and correct problem behavior in a dog-friendly way.

Whether you are a new dog owner or your dog is one of many you have owned, I hope this book will help you enjoy a rewarding relationship with your pet.

— Chapter 1 —

Training... Who Needs It?

Every dog needs training. Pet dogs do not need to perform a perfect competition "front and finish" when you call them to come to you, but they need to know how to come to you every time you call. They do not need to walk at heel perfectly, but when on leash, they need to know how to keep from choking themselves and from pulling their owner along behind them. Training means teaching. Good teachers understand the special needs of their students and develop a good relationship with them based upon mutual respect and clearly defined rules.

Training helps make it clear to your dog who is the leader. It might surprise you to find out how happy your dog will be to have you take control. He will no longer feel like he has the responsibility of taking care of you. Instead, he will learn that you have the responsibility of taking care of him. That is how it should be. Living with you suddenly becomes a whole lot easier for your dog because he knows his place in the "pack".

If you do not become a leader, normal canine behaviors such as biting, barking, chewing and jumping can become behavior problems. As a leader, you make the rules so your dog knows when his behavior is inappropriate. Just teaching and using a few obedience commands ("sit", "down", "leave it", "stay", "come") can help solve many behaviorial problems. Dogs misbehave for many different reasons, but at the core of most unwanted behavior is a lack of training. You will see a change in your dog for the better when you start to train him.

Training helps strengthen the bond between you and your dog. He will look forward to his training time and the playtime afterwards. When you work together as a pack (or team), it gives your dog his role in the pack. The more you and your dog work together, the more you will understand your dog. Dogs are thinking animals and they need to keep their brains busy. A bored dog is an unhappy dog and an unhappy dog usually develops behavior problems. Training stimulates your dog's mind; the more he learns, the more intelligent he becomes. A lot of dog owners find that a good way to play and have fun with their dogs and keep their minds stimulated is with dog sports. Today there are many sports from which to choose; there is a sport for every dog, purebred or mutt out there and they all have one thing in common: they begin with basic obedience training.

It takes time, patience and consistency to train a dog. An understanding of simple dog psychology and behavior makes the process easier for you and your dog. Dogs don't learn new behaviors overnight. In a rush to stop problem behaviors, owners tend to expect too much too fast from their dogs. They say, "I've tried everything and my dog just won't stop (chewing, barking, digging, etc.)". These owners try one thing and if it doesn't work in a day or two, they try something else. This confuses the dog and makes it very hard for him to learn. Try one technique for two weeks before trying something new.

Who needs training? All dogs need training in order to learn how to live with humans and be good canine citizens. Start training your dog or puppy as soon as you get her. Nobody wants to be around a dog who hasn't learned good manners.

— Chapter 2 —

Understanding Dog Behavior

Domestic dogs have been a part of human civilization for about 10,000 years. Dogs are so much a part of our lives that we take them for granted. We might think that we understand our dogs, but unless we make an effort to learn about dog behavior, we are relying on our limited personal experience and our subjective perception of dogs. What we know about dogs is often filtered through our human minds, which interpret dog behavior in human terms. In other words, we construct stories about what we think our dogs are thinking. When owners say things like, "My dog is doing that because he's mad at me," or "He knows he's been bad. He looks guilty," they are interpreting their dog's behavior in human terms. Trainers call it anthropomorphizing. Problems arise when we try to read our dogs' minds and interpret their emotions. Owners who react as they would to a human interaction use ineffective methods to correct their dog's behavior.

One should not treat dogs like people. Dogs do not think and react like people; they think and react like dogs. Some people enjoy thinking of their dogs as their "babies" and try to make them happy by giving them whatever they want, whenever they demand it. However, if we treat our dogs like human children, we can expect our dogs to develop behavior problems.

Dogs need instruction and guidance. Dogs are happiest when a human is in charge. Most dogs know they are not suitable leader material, but dogs are social animals. Their ancestors lived in packs and our dogs still retain some of that pack mentality. A pack needs a leader to function. The leader makes the rules and other pack members submit to his demands or suffer serious consequences. There is no such thing as a dog democracy. Dogs need to know their place in the social hierarchy of the pack. The human family is the domestic dog's pack. If you do not act like a leader, your dog will. I know a woman whose dog, Copper (not his real name), has trained her well. He is clearly the leader of the pack and the humans in the family submit to his demands. If his owner is eating chicken, Copper barks until she gives him a piece of her chicken. If Copper refuses to eat his dog food, she gives him human food. Copper does not like his dog bed, so he sleeps in his owner's bed. If she wants him to get off the bed, he growls at her, so she leaves him alone. Copper does not like one of her children. When he growls at the child, the child leaves him alone. Everyone in the family does what Copper tells them to do! His owner created this situation out of "love" for her dog. She loves him, so she gives him whatever he wants. Because pack leaders control food, sleeping areas, and other valuable resources, in Copper's view of the world, his owner put him in charge. Dogs only do what works. If his owner ignored Copper's barking, he would eventually stop. If barking was not a way to get chicken, he would not bark while the family was having dinner. If his owner taught Copper to get off her bed when she asked him to, he would learn that she makes the decisions about who sleeps in her bed. A human *must* be the leader of the pack, must make the decisions, control the resources and set the rules.

Dogs are individuals, but often owners become frustrated with a dog because he is not like other dogs they have owned. They say, "Our old dog, Rex, never acted like that. There's something wrong with *this* dog." Dogs raised under seemingly identical conditions do not behave identically. It is impossible to reproduce the same conditions and experiences for every dog you own. There are critical periods in a dog's development. Puppies that are not given opportunities at critical stages are often at a disadvantage. They learn some things more slowly or sometimes not at all. For instance, there is a time during a puppy's development (around eight to nine weeks of age) that is the best time to teach him to retrieve. If that window of opportunity closes, the dog can still learn to retrieve, but it takes longer for him to learn. If he is not a natural retriever, he may never be interested in retrieving. Puppies taken from their mothers too soon have difficulty getting along with other dogs. When they play with people or dogs, they do not know how to play without biting too hard. Puppies taken from their mothers too late are often fearful of strangers, strange places, and new situations. This fear can remain throughout adulthood.

— Chapter 3 —

Exchanging Body Language with Your Dog

Videotaped training sessions of dog trainers and dog owners show that trainers give much more feedback to dogs compared to owners. Feedback is a non-stop flow of verbal and physical communication between trainer and dog. A good trainer tells the dog what she wants him to do. She praises him when he is doing a good job and encourages him when he needs it. She warns him if he is about to make a mistake, and tells him when he is wrong. Owners typically give their dog a command and praise if he performs correctly. They rarely give enthusiastic praise or offer verbal encouragement to give the dog confidence or to let him know when he is on the right track. Saying "Almost!" when your dog almost has it right, or "Oops!" when he makes a mistake helps him learn new commands more quickly.

Most people wait for their dog to do something wrong and then correct him, rather than praise him when he is doing something right. If your dog is lying down quietly at your side while you are watching TV, reinforce that behavior with praise or a treat. Do not wait until your dog is doing something *wrong* to communicate with him. Let him know when he is doing something *right*! The more you reward a behavior, the more your dog performs that behavior. The more you reinforce good behavior, the faster your dog learns good behavior.

Part of effective feedback includes an ability to anticipate your dog's next move. Dog "whisperers" who seem to control dogs or modify behavior telepathically work their magic by establishing communication primarily with body language, and by keeping a constant flow of feedback between themselves and the dogs they are working with. Dog trainers have a mental database of dog body language and behavior gained by years of watching hundreds of dogs. However, anyone can learn to read dog body language. Dogs use body language to communicate with each other and with us. They are aware of the slightest movements that we make. Because of this, visual signals are easier for them to learn than understanding verbal commands.

Dogs "telegraph" what they are about to do next and you can use that to your advantage. When working with your dog, really watch him. Dogs rarely do things suddenly and without meaning. A dog that is about to stand up from a sitting position shifts his weight and moves his body slightly forward before his rear end comes off the floor. If you told your dog to "stay" and watch for this, you can anticipate when the dog is going to get up and use that information to decide what to do next. You could use body language by leaning or walking forward to prevent him from getting up, or you could give him the "stay" command again in case he forgot. Better yet, you can release him from the "stay" *before he gets up* and then reward him for holding the "stay". You will have set the dog up for success. Rewarding and reinforcing the *right* behavior is more effective than correcting and punishing the *wrong* behavior. Remember, catch your dog doing something right and reward it!

A dog's body language can help you understand how he might be feeling — aggressive, submissive, playful, relaxed or focused. Dogs act differently when they are upset about something or if they want another dog or human to settle down, or when they want to reassure others. Dogs watch our behavior for clues about what we are going to do next. How many of us have thought, *I have a really smart dog. How does he know I'm going to the store?* To your dog, it is pretty obvious that you are not going to work or to school. Your grooming

A dog's body language can help you understand how he might be feeling. Wesley's ears are forward, but flat and his forehead is wrinkled. He is unsure of what is going to happen next.

routine, your clothes, the way you smell, the way you walk, and the expression on your face are different. Your dog notices your signals. But do you notice the signals your dog gives you? Animals that live in groups, like dogs, wolves, and people, need ways to cooperate, resolve conflicts, and communicate with each other. If you are like most people, you did not notice your dog turn his head and lick his nose when you were irritated and told him to get out of your way. Maybe he yawned and sniffed the floor, or turned his back to you. These and other behaviors that appear out of context are called displacement behaviors and are often signs of stress. Many dog signals happen so quickly that if we are not looking for them, we will not see them. Try mimicking dog body language to communicate with a dog that is uncomfortable, nervous or excited.

Turn Your Head: A dog that is nervous or uncomfortable might turn his head to the side if you lean over him or if you walk too quickly toward him.

In order to accurately interpret your dog's behavior, look at the whole dog from head to tail. Sometimes when the white's of a dog's eyes look like half moons the dog is very stressed, frightened and could bite.

Does your dog get nervous when you want to take his picture? Notice if he turns his head when you point the camera at him. Dogs look away to avoid eye contact. Staring, in dog language, is extremely rude. Many dog fights begin that way. Use the Turn Your Head signal to try and calm your dog or to help reassure a dog that is barking or growling at you.

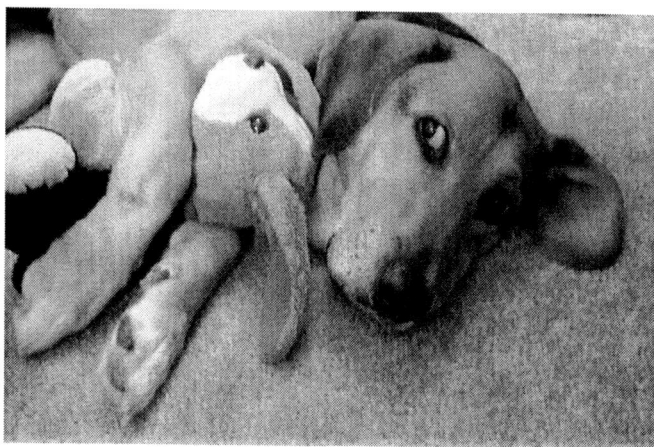

You can see the whites of Theo's eyes and his brow is a little furrowed, but his ears are relaxed and he is laying comfortably on his side. He might be alert to (and a little concerned about) what his humans are doing, but he is not frightened or dangerous.

Sit Down, Turn Away: Sometimes dogs turn their back to other dogs or people to ask them to calm down. If your dog thinks you are mad at him, he might use this signal. If you jerk on his leash or run up to him too fast, he might turn away to calm you down. Turning your back on a jumping dog is a good way to let him know you want him to settle down.

Stand Still: Smart little dogs use this when greeting big dogs. They don't move a muscle until the big dog has finished sniffing them all over. If they move too quickly, they might get bitten.

Yawn: Dogs yawn when they are tired or bored, when they are uneasy about something, and to calm themselves or others. A good place for you to use this signal to calm you dog might be at the veterinary office. Sometimes dogs yawn and turn their head to the side.

Step In-between: Your dog might use this move to separate you from another dog or person. Dogs are experts at conflict resolution and if you are arguing with someone, your dog will stand in between you and the person you are arguing with to try and calm you both down.

Dogs use their whole body to communicate. You can tell what a dog is feeling by the way he holds his tail, his ears, his eyes, his mouth and his body.

Dog breed variations can make it difficult to read a dog's body language. It is even difficult for other dogs to read and sometimes misunderstandings result. Many times, dogs with these "handicaps" compensate for them. For example, a dog with no tail will furiously wag his whole rear end. By the way, it is a myth that a wagging tail equals a happy dog. Most dogs wag their tails when they are happy, but many people have been bitten by a dog that was wagging its tail! A wagging tail just means a dog is excited. Dogs wag their tails fast or slow, held high or low. The position as well as the speed mean something different. When dogs greet each other, one dog may hold his tail stiff and wag it slowly. He wants the other dog to know that he wants to be in charge. There could be a fight if the other dog holds his tail the same as the first dog. In polite dog society, one dog will often submit by breaking off the contact or lowering his tail or body, or inviting the other dog to play by bowing. Dogs that hold their tails stiff and wag them very fast during greeting are not usually threatening each other, but whenever unfamiliar dogs meet, carefully watch both so that any potential conflict can be interupted and a fight prevented before it starts. To understand how a dog is feeling, look at the whole dog, not just the tail. A dog's ears are forward and "perked up" when he is alert and unafraid. An alert dog will also lean his body forward slightly. When he is afraid, a dog's ears are flat back and close to his head. His body will lean back and away from the source of fear or he might crouch low to the ground with his head down and his tail tucked between his legs.

Crouch down (or bend at the knees) rather than bend over to greet or reach for small dogs and puppies. Bending over is threatening to many dogs of all sizes. Often dogs will back away or refuse to come to someone who bends over.

With a little effort, you can learn to read your dog's body language and be one step ahead of him. If you are interested in learning more, there are many books available about interpreting dog body language.

— Chapter 4 —

Reward Your Dog

    Dogs are opportunists. They do what works to get what they want. If dogs were not that way, our ancestors might never have formed the unique relationship that we humans share with our dogs. Hungry dogs would have been attracted by the smell of human food and refuse. At first, humans may have only appreciated the warmth of dog fur or taste of dog meat, but at some point they learned to appreciate the dogs' barks that warned them of intruders, and to appreciate the dogs' skill at tracking game. Mutual benefit is still what motivates the relationship between people and dogs Whether or not your dog will understand how you want him to behave has nothing to do with love and a willingness to please. It depends upon whether he has learned what you want him to do, and on his physical ability and his motivation to want to do it. Dog owners tend to overlook the importance of motivation, but without it, there is no learning.

Without motivation, your dog will not do what you what him to do. Motivation in a dog has been compared to the gasoline in a car. No matter how well your car runs, without gas you will never know how well it runs. Most people think that the secret to a well-behaved dog lies in having the "right" training collar and using it the "right" way. That is not true. A properly motivated dog can be trained with no collar and leash.

Many things motivate dogs and the motivation you provide has to be stronger than the dog's motivation to do something else. What motivates your dog depends somewhat on genetics. Think about the job your dog was bred to do and look for appropriate rewards. If your dog was bred to retrieve, a game of fetch might be a good reward. All dogs are motivated by food. Many owners refuse to use food to train their dog. They believe their dog will never obey them unless they have food. That is not true and those owners rarely see how well their dogs can perform.

Rewards are what motivated dogs work for. Rewards can be food, toys, play, praise, petting, or whatever you know makes your dog's tail wag. If your dog would rather play ball than anything else in the world, tossing the ball to him is a great reward. Find out what it is your dog loves and use that as a reward. Rewards are very powerful and have a direct effect on your dog's behavior. Use them to reinforce good behavior. The type of reward, the amount, how good it is (from the dog's point of view), how often it is given, and the timing of the delivery all have an effect on how well your dog will learn. Slightly hungry dogs work better for food rewards. Dogs perform better for tastier food rewards. A great reward given all the time begins to be not so great after a while.

The best treats must be tasty to dogs. Examples include freeze-dried liver, canned chicken, tuna or cat food (yes, cat food is a safe and healthy treat for dogs), hot dogs, or anything that your dog loves. Dogs work best for tiny bits of treat. Some dogs are happy to work for dry dog food. If your dog is overweight, or you are concerned about adding more calories, use a portion of his food ration for training rewards.

Timing is critical to training. For a reward to be effective in reinforcing a desired behavior, it must be delivered within two or three seconds of the behavior. Any longer than three seconds and the dog has gone on to think about (or actually do) other things, any one of which you might not want reinforced.

Some examples of ready-made treats your dog might enjoy.

Example: An owner asks his dog to sit. The dog sits. The owner goes to the kitchen, gets a treat out the treat jar and offers it to the dog, who has followed him into the kitchen. The owner thinks he reinforced sitting behavior, when in fact he reinforced coming to the kitchen. A verbal or mechanical marker (a whistle, a clicker or a one-syllable word, "Good", for example) should be used to let the dog know that a reward is coming, even if it is not coming immediately. This marker or "bridge" can buy a few precious seconds for owners who are a little slow in getting a treat out of their pocket. It is a promise to pay and becomes almost as powerful as the actual reward.

Punishment also requires good timing. When people think of punishment, they think of corporal punishment—spanking, slapping, hitting, or kicking. But punishment does not have to involve pain or physically touching the dog. Punishment is in the eyes of the punished, not the punisher. What you consider punishment may not be what your dog considers punishment. For example, some people recommend squirting a dog with water from a water bottle to make him stop barking. If your dog loves being squirted with water and thinks you are playing a game with him, it is not punishment. Just talking to them in a loud, deep, stern voice is punishment to most pet dogs. Physical punishment may make the punisher feel better, but it is rarely effective in training. Whale, dolphin and seal trainers cannot physically punish their animals, and yet they train them to do (or not do) many amazing things. You do not need to physically punish a dog in order to change his behavior.

Owners typically use physical punishment during housetraining. An owner comes home and finds dog poop behind the couch. The owner grabs the dog, shows him the poop, scolds him, maybe spanks him or puts his nose in the poop, and puts him outside. Dogs live in the present and correcting them after the fact is never effective. You must catch them in the act, calmly show them the proper place to go, and reward them when they go there. Otherwise, you must ignore it. You dog may look "guilty" when you come home and find poop behind the couch, but he is not feeling guilty about pooping there. He just knows that when you and dog poop are together in the same room, you become angry and bad things happen to him. In dog language, it is proper to show submission, sometimes by rolling over belly up and urinating, to appease a more dominant, angry individual. The angry dog accepts this as a "win" and leaves. But humans who do not speak "dog" ignore the appeasement signals. Unlike dogs, submissive urination makes humans angrier, and they continue their attack without mercy. Imagine how confusing that is for the dog! Humans seem unpredictable and cruel. A better solution to the housetraining problem is to keep the dog in a kennel, or safely restricted in some other fashion, when he cannot be supervised until he is housetrained, and reward him when he does his "business" outside.

Remember, dogs think in the present. You must catch your dog in the act in order to reward or correct.

— Chapter 5 —

Make Time for Training

If you have planned well, you got your puppy or dog during a period when you have time to spend with him. A puppy needs your full time attention for several months. If you adopt an older dog, spend several days giving him your full attention so he can adapt to a new home and your routine.

Some dog owners dream of having the real-life equivalent of Lassie but many owners do not have the time or knowledge to train their dog to that degree. Animal actors are highly trained dogs, trained by people who do nothing but train dogs all day. If a very highly trained dog is your goal, that is fine but most people just want their dog to sit, come when called, walk nicely on a leash, and have good manners. Finding the time and motivation to train those basic behaviors can be difficult for some people. Owners might fool themselves into thinking that a puppy will grow out of any bad behavior and that they do not need to find time in their busy schedule for training. But instead, the puppy's behavior just gets worse as the dog gets older. Sometimes the dog becomes uncontrollable. That is usually when owners decide they need to quickly train the dog or get rid of the dog.

It is much easier to start training when your dog is a puppy so he does not get the chance to practice bad behaviors as he grows up, but dogs of any age can be trained with consistency and patience. The old saying, "You can't teach an old dog new tricks" is just not true.

Even the busiest person can find five minutes once or twice each day to train their dog. Dogs learn best with short, daily training sessions. You can easily fit dog training into your daily routine. While waiting for the coffee to brew, you can practice "sit" a few times. Ask your dog to "sit" or "lie down" before you give him his food bowl, before he goes outside, or before he comes inside. You can practice "stay" while you are watching TV. Think of other ways you might incorporate training into your daily routine. Every interaction with your dog is an opportunity for training.

Dog training does not end with the accomplishment of a command (like "sit" or "stay") or with completion of a training class. Training goes on for the life of the dog. If you do not practice, your dog will forget what he learned. When dogs are first learning a new command, daily practice is necessary. Consistency is important and only one person should train the dog. When your dog can obey a command most of the time, teach him that "sit" means "sit" no matter where or when or who tells him to sit. To do that you must train in a variety of places and under a variety of circumstances. This is also the time to teach other family members how to give the dog commands. When the dog reliably obeys most of the time (80% to 90% of the time) in a variety of places, he needs only a minimum of practice to retain what he has learned.

Train your dog several times a day for about five to fifteen minutes each session. Just like with playing a musical instrument, practice makes perfect. The more you train, the better trained your dog will be. In fact, training never really stops. But do not let that discourage you. Training should be fun! If either one of you is not having fun, stop. Take a break and try again later. Forget about any frustrations or setbacks from the last training session. It is important to play with your dog after each training session. Do something he likes to do. He will begin to associate training, and you, with all good things.

Try practicing training a new behavior first without your dog. Do everything you would do with the dog; imagine how you will hold the leash, practice dispensing treats or other rewards, practice what you will say to the dog and when. You might feel silly at first, but rehearsing without the dog will make you aware of any sequence or timing problems that you need to work on. If you train a new behavior without practicing it alone first, you risk making mistakes and confusing the dog. Your dog will learn more quickly if you are not learning at the same time. If you still feel silly, think of yourself as a teacher preparing a lesson plan. A good teacher does not go to class without first having prepared a lesson plan.

— Chapter 6 —

Housetraining... "P" is for Puppy

Do you remember how long it took you before you were potty trained? As a mom, I can tell you it does not happen overnight. It takes vigilance, encouragement, patience, praise and bribery. Just when it seems like diapers would be part of the cost of a college education, the light seems to come on in a toddler's head, and all that work pays off. He or she is potty trained!

Training your puppy to use a special "toilet area" is a lot like that. It can take months before he can be trusted not to make mistakes. The more diligent and supportive you are, the faster he will learn. Your goal should be to avoid letting your puppy make a mistake. It's a lot easier to teach a puppy what he *should do* than to teach him what he *should not do*. Although I assume you are going to train your puppy to go outdoors, this method works for any kind of housetraining—paper, litter box or outdoors, and will work for adult dogs too.

It is important to put your puppy on a feeding schedule. Write down the time he eats and the time he poops. When you have a daily record of times, then you will know what time you need to take him to his toilet area. You will also need to take him out about 10 minutes after he has a drink of water. Take your puppy out after a nap. After he has been playing, he will need to potty, too. Just like little kids, puppies get so excited about playing they do not want to stop and go to the bathroom. That is when accidents happen.

Puppies are easily distracted, so leaving him outside by himself just will not work. You need to stay with him so he can learn what it is you want him to do. You might want him to hurry up and go potty, but your puppy would rather play. Be patient, but help your puppy focus on the task at hand by telling him something like, "(Puppy), go potty." (use his name and whatever word you want to use to make him go.) When he goes, tell him, "good puppy potty" and give him a treat. If you are consistent and patient, your puppy will learn to go potty when you tell him! Some day when it is raining or cold outside, or you are in a hurry, you will be glad you taught him that command.

Remember, if your puppy has an accident, it's not the puppy's fault. It is your fault. You were not paying close enough attention. If your puppy makes a mistake, ignore it. *Never rub his nose in it or spank him*. That will only make him lose his trust in you, and hide his mistakes from you. It is a lot better to find a mistake out in the open than behind the couch! If you catch him in the act, interrupt him by saying something like, "Aaa Aaa" or "Oh, no!" Pick him up and carry him to his potty area and tell him to go there. Only correct your puppy if you catch him in the act. Otherwise, say nothing. Clean up the mess when your puppy is not looking. Make sure you clean the spot with an enzyme cleaning product that neutralizes the odor. Soap is not enough. If you do not remove the odor, the puppy will want to go there again.

All puppies are different. How long it will take before your puppy is completely housetrained depends on how attentive you are and how smart he is and how willing he is to learn. It is not appropriate to ask an eight-week-old puppy to control his bladder for more than an hour. Expecting him to learn bladder control in a few days in unrealistic. Do not be disappointed if your puppy is eight or nine months old before you can trust him. And, do not get mad at him if he has a setback after you think he should be trained. Just be patient. Your puppy will be telling you when he needs to go out before you know it!

— Chapter 7 —

Crate Training

A portable kennel, also called a crate, is a great place for your dog to call his own in your house. They are also convenient for traveling. Dogs like to hang their heads out of car windows, but your dog is safer in his crate. On long trips or stays at a boarding kennel, it can be comforting for your dog to have his familiar "house" with him. A crate should be just large enough for your dog to stand up and turn around comfortably. Crates make housetraining easier, unless the crate is too large. Dogs naturally do not soil their sleeping area, but if the crate is too large, the dog will use a portion of the crate to relieve himself and never learn bowel and bladder control.

To train your dog to go into his crate, put a few treats in the back of it. When he goes in for the treats, praise him. Don't shut the door. If he won't go all the way in for the treats, put them just inside the door. After a few times of going in and coming out, shut the door with the dog inside for just a few seconds. Open the door and praise him. Let the dog get used to being confined by slowly increasing the time he is inside with the door closed. When he is comfortable going in and out of the crate, add a command like, "crate" or "go to bed" when he goes inside. Don't use the crate to punish the dog. He should associate it only with comfortable things.

Crates are useful, but unfortunately, they are sometimes used as long-term confinement. Too often a dog is crated for his entire life as a substitute for training. Crating any dog in a portable kennel, but especially a puppy, for eight hours per day and expecting him to be happy is unrealistic not to mention cruel! If you must crate your dog, arrange for him to have out-of-crate-breaks with exercise and play, provide stimulating toys in the crate, and give him something to chew away any frustration. Crating should be temporary until your dog has learned enough manners to be trusted alone in the house. Then, unless you install a doggie door or train your dog to paper or to a litter box, you still should arrange for your dog to relieve himself outdoors and have a brief playtime.

Why is confinement for eight hours too long? Simply put, eight hours in a crate is too long for a puppy for the same reason that eight hours in a crate would be too long for you. It is tedious, boring and lonely. A puppy will need to potty during those eight hours and cannot hold it. Social isolation and sensory deprivation contribute to behavior problems. To a curious and active puppy, eight hours of being locked up can be frustrating and distressing. A common problem described by owners when a puppy is finally released from the crate is that "he goes nuts." The puppy is so excited and hyperactive that the owner resorts to punishment (verbal or physical) to make the puppy settle down. It can become a vicious cycle of confinement, isolation, frustration, hyper-excitability, punishment, confinement, isolation. Both the dog and the owner are frustrated.

Adult dogs with nothing to do will usually sleep for hours during the day, but a puppy crated for eight hours is bored, no matter how many toys you put in the crate. Puppies need attention and a variety of stimuli. Dogs are social animals and need contact with other dogs or humans to be well-balanced, happy, good canine citizens. Unfortunately, many people don't understand the needs of puppies before they acquire them. If you are unable to come home during the day to let the puppy out, or do not have a trusted person who can do it for

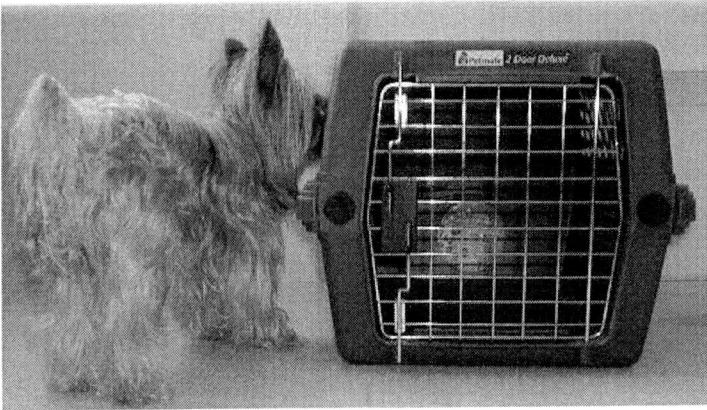

Cozy's crate is just large enough for her to stand up and turn around comfortably in it.

you, and cannot afford a puppy day care, then it is important that the remainder of the day be spent training, exercising and playing with the puppy. If the puppy is crated at night in addition to during the day, the total number of hours of confinement is well over eight hours.

Many dogs are left alone and crated for eight hours or more every day. That doesn't mean it the best choice or in the best interest of the dogs. Locking your dog in a crate should be a temporary measure to keep your dog and your belongings safe in the house until he is trained and can be trusted alone.

— Chapter 8 —

Understanding Collars and Leashes

    With so many choices for collars, leashes, and harnesses, it is easy for owners to become confused about which is best. Some people use a particular collar because "We've always used that on our dogs." Others buy a new leash because it is popular with other owners. Trainers have their own preferences, too. For the health, safety and well-being of your dog, please do not go out and buy a special training collar without having been instructed in its proper use. A dog's temperament must be taken into consideration when using any special training equipment. Unless a dog trainer or handler has shown you how to use a choke collar, prong collar, shock collar, or head halter, the only training equipment you need for your dog is his everyday buckle collar or harness, and a non-retractable leash. If you have a small toy breed or a very young puppy, a harness is better than a collar. Toy breeds that are prone to collapsing trachea should wear a harness instead of a collar in order to prevent any unintentional damage to the trachea. Very young puppies are sometimes afraid and struggle against the strange and unfamiliar tightness around their necks. They fear it because they do not understand it. They will struggle less against a harness. With a harness, the leash is also farther from a puppy's mouth and he is not tempted to chew on it.

Yorkshire Terriers Zada and Azrael are toy breeds prone to collapsing trachea. They wear harnesses instead of collars in order to prevent any unintentional damage to their necks.

The buckle collar is your dog's everyday collar. It holds his rabies and ID tags. To fit your dog to a buckle collar, measure your dog's neck with a tape measure or a piece of string long enough to go around the circumference of your dog's neck. Collars are usually sized by length. It is a good idea to take the dog or the measuring string with you when you buy a collar. The width of the collar and the buckle should be appropriate for the size of your dog. A collar that is too wide will be uncomfortable. The collar should be snug, but you should be able to slip your finger comfortably between the collar and your dog's neck. It should not be so loose that the dog can slip out of the collar or allow for the dog to get caught on something.

To fit your dog to a harness, measure your dog's girth starting from underneath and behind his front legs, around to the top at his withers (shoulder blades). Chest size is usually about half this measurement, except in breeds with large chests, like bulldogs. Harnesses are usually sized by girth, but not always. For comfort, the width of the harness should be appropriate to the size of your

Side view of a harness with the leash attachment on the chest strap. Bonnie wears her everyday collar in addition to the harness because the collar holds her ID tags.

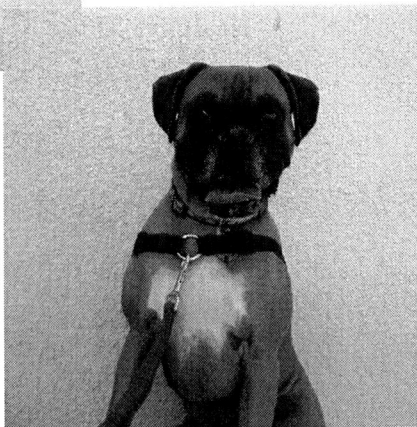

Calvin is wearing a harness with the leash attachment on the chest strap. It is designed to prevent him from pulling on the leash by redirecting forward movement.

dog. The leash attachment is on the top of most harnesses, and on the chest strap of others. The latter is designed to prevent pulling by redirecting the dog's forward movement.

A six-foot long nylon, cotton or leather leash of a width and clip size suitable for the size of your dog is all you need for walking your dog and for most obedience work. A lot of information is shared between dog and handler through the leash. A heavy leash makes it hard for your dog to feel you at the other end. A leash should be just strong enough to prevent the dog from breaking it if he pulls hard enough. Sometimes the breaking strength of a leash is printed on the sales tag. A leash with a listed breaking strength of 500 pounds can withstand just under 500 pounds of force. A 15-foot or longer leash is convenient when training your dog to come when you call, especially when they are still easily distracted. Retractable leashes are popular but not suitable for training.

The large plastic handles are bulky and get in the way during training. It is impossible to hold the leash properly. Retractable leashes were designed for dogs that are already trained and well behaved.

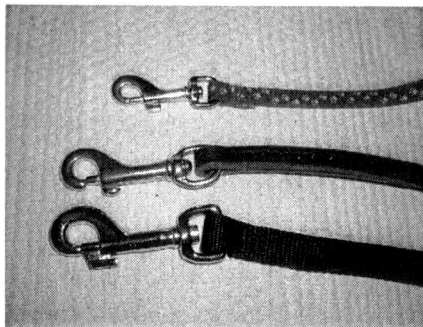

Use a six-foot long nylon, cotton, or leather leash of a width, weight and clip size suitable for the size of your dog.

The following collars are considered special training equipment and should be used *only* under supervision of a trainer who knows the proper technique for use. Used incorrectly, these collars can cause dog to suffer emotional trauma, as well as physical damage to their vertebrae and throat. Your trainer will decide if any of these collars are or are not appropriate for your dog.

Slip collars: These collars, sometimes called "choke chains", are made of chain or nylon and slip over the dog's head. They have one ring at each end and the chain slips through one ring, forming a loop. It is important to buy a well-made collar. Chain links must slip freely, both when tightening and loosening the slip. Inexpensive collars have links that can "hang up" and not slip freely. To determine the proper size of chain slip collar for your dog, add two inches to your dog's neck measurement. The collar should slip comfortably over the widest part of the dog's head. The size of the links should be in proportion to the size of your dog. Slip collars are not designed to choke a dog to prevent him from pulling on the leash. A dog will continue to pull against the leash no matter how much the collar tightens around his neck. A properly executed leash correction with a slip collar causes the chain to quickly tighten around the dog's neck for only a second or less before the slack is returned to the chain. Slip collars are unpopular with many dog trainers, but are still the training collar of choice for others. The American Kennel Club does not consider slip collars special training equipment and they are allowed to be used in the show ring. Slip collars should never be left on an unsupervised dog or used as an everyday collar because of the danger of strangulation. Remember—do not use a slip collar unless you have been shown how to use it properly.

A variation of the slip collar is a "snap-around" collar. It snaps around the neck rather than slipping over the head, and consists of a swivel snap, a "floating" ring and a stationary ring. It can be used as a training collar and as an everyday collar depending on which ring the snap is fastened to. You can size a snap-around collar by measuring your dog's neck size just behind the ears and adding one inch.

Limited choke: These collars slip over the head. They have two rings like a slip chain, but one ring is fastened so that it can move only a few inches. When the collar tightens, it can tighten only to the size of the dog's neck. It is considered safer than a slip collar. The martingale (or greyhound) collar is a type of limited choke collar that has a loop of material between the rings that can lay flat or be used as a handle.

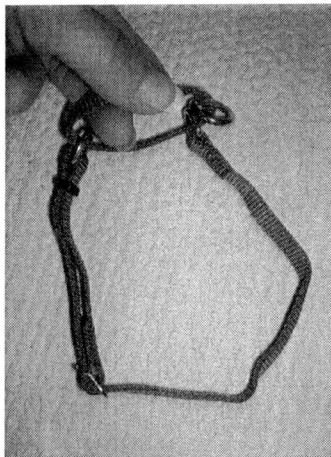

A limited slip or martingale collar

Prong collars: Also called pinch collars, they are made of interlocking prongs that rest against the dog's neck. When the prongs are pulled tight, they apply pressure to the dog's neck. Prong collars have a limited slip so the prongs cannot tighten more than the size of the dog's neck. When a dog is considerably more powerful than his owner or cannot be controlled by other means, a prong collar can be helpful. To fit a prong collar, measure your dog's neck behind the ears. Unlike a slip collar, a prong collar should fit snugly around the dog's neck—not too tight, but not too loose. It should rest higher on the neck, just tight enough that the collar does not fall down around the lowest part of the neck. These collars are adjustable and links can be added or removed as needed. Prong collars should not be used on all dogs. A dog's temperament must be taken into consideration when using any training equipment. Dogs that are sensitive, and cringe or crouch from a verbal reprimand, should not be trained with a slip or prong collar. Owners that are impatient or that have quick or short tempers should not use a prong or slip collar on their dog.

Head Collars: Also known as halters, head collars are relatively new compared to other equipment and some people love these. A head collar has a nose loop and a strap that fastens around the back of a dog's head. The leash attachment is underneath the dog's chin. It looks similar to a head harness for a horse. Head collars work on the principal that where the head goes, the rest of the dog must go. Head collars bother most dogs and they must be trained to accept them. The nose loop applies pressure when

Jasmine is wearing a head collar or halter.

the leash tightens and turns the dog's head in the direction of the leash. Like other training collars, you should be properly trained in its use to avoid physical damage to the dog. There are several brands of head collars and some dogs are more comfortable in one style than in another. Because every brand fits differently, it is best to take your dog with you for sizing.

Electronic Collars: Electronic collars, also called shock or remote training collars, are more sophisticated compared to those of twenty years ago and have settings for various degrees of stimulation (some levels so low that the dog can hardly feel it) from vibration or tone to several levels of shock. The transmitter is a handheld device that looks similar to a remote control for a toy car. A receiver with two metal points is mounted on the inside of the plastic collar. The points make contact with the dog's neck and deliver the stimulation when the signal is received from the transmitter. Electronic collars are enjoying a resurgence in popularity and are widely available to the public. The quality of electronic components, and the reliability and the safety of the collar are directly proportional to the price of the collar. If you think you would like to train with an electronic collar, there are trainers who can teach you how to use them. Please do not buy one at your local pet store and begin "training" your dog with it. Before using an electronic collar, you need to know when it is effective to train with one, have a well thought-out training plan, and have good timing. Electronic collars are a controversial topic among trainers. Some feel that they should never be used. Others believe the collars are effective as a last resort or for training commands like "come" or "heel" off leash, for example. Still other trainers think they are suitable for everything. Use of electronic collars is forbidden by law in the United Kingdom and a few other countries.

Remember, if you use any special training collar for your dog, it must not be used as his everyday collar. He will need a comfortable buckle collar to hold his tags in addition to the training collar.

— Chapter 9 —

Walking Nicely on a Leash

Teach your dog to walk by your side. This is easiest with puppies because puppies naturally want to be with you. It will work with older dogs, too, but it might take a little longer and you will need more patience. This method does not use any leash correction. This means you will not jerk or pull hard on your dog's collar or harness. Remember, a 6 foot long nylon, cotton or leather leash is best for leash training. Do not use a retractable leash. Practice in the house or someplace where your dog has little or no distractions. You want his full attention.

Put the leash on your dog and have a treat in your hand. With the dog on your left side, start forward with your left foot. Walk forward quickly and say, "(Puppy), let's go." Use **your dog's name** before "let's go." This lets him know that you are talking to him and not somebody else. Don't use the command "come". Chapter 10 will explain more about that. If your dog follows you without lunging ahead, say "good dog!" Give him a treat. Slow down and stop walking. Tell him, "Puppy, sit." You want him to sit next to you at your left side. If your dog does not already know how to sit, teach him by holding the treat above his nose and moving it backward so he has to tilt his head back to see it. As you move it back, he will naturally sit down. Make sure you are not holding the treat too high or he will jump up to get it instead of sit down. When he sits, say "good dog!" and give him the treat. Pet him and tell him what a clever dog he is. Then, say, "puppy, let's go," and start walking again. As long as he is walking with you, not ahead of you, tell him he is a good dog. After a few steps, stop and tell him to sit.

You might have to lure him with the treat several times before he understands what it is you want him to do. Eventually, he will start to sit every time you stop walking. Walk quickly when you are teaching your dog to walk with you. Slow down before you stop walking so he knows what you are planning to do.

Eleusis demonstrates 'heeling'. She pays close attention to Kate (her owner) and stays in the same position at her side no matter which way Kate turns.

If your dog wants to run ahead of you, all you have to do is turn in the opposite direction and keep walking. If the dog pulls on the leash, resist the temptation to pull back. A dog naturally pulls against a strong, opposing force.

That is why dogs are used to pull sleds. A dog cannot pull if you do not give him something to pull against. Get his attention by calling his name and clapping your hand on your leg. If he does not want to follow, stop. Let him think about it a minute. Start walking again and encourage him to follow. When he follows you, say, "Good dog!" and give him a treat. Whenever he starts to pull ahead of you, walk the other way. Don't forget to practice stopping and sitting, too. Do whatever you need to do to encourage him to follow you without pulling on the leash. If he absolutely will not budge, even if you are bribing him to with a treat, stop the training and try again later.

Practice this exercise several times a day, every day. Do not practice in the same place all the time or your dog will learn to walk with your there, but not anywhere else. As your dog gets better, move the training outdoors where there is just a little more distraction. Be patient. There are many interesting things to smell outdoors and you will have to make yourself the most interesting thing in your dog's world. If you cannot get your dog's attention outdoors, even by offering him better treats, give a gentle tug on the leash when you say, "let's go." Or, practice with less distractions.

Even with lots of distractions, owner Joni is still the most interesting thing in Bonnie's environment.

A tennis ball tied to a string is a good way to practice leash walking without your dog. The ball should be about an inch so off the ground. Pretend the ball is your dog. Try to be smooth enough when you are walking the "dog" to keep the ball hanging straight down by your side, not swinging back and forth. It will give you an idea of what your dog feels when he is at the end of the leash!

Here's a word about off-leash training: off-leash training is part of advanced obedience training. If you show your dog in obedience, agility, or other dog sports, your dog will be required to work off leash but, in an urban environment, it is dangerous for your dog to be off leash. Most municipalities have leash laws that require your dog to be leashed when in public. Part of responsible dog ownership means obeying the legal requirements for your pet. Responsible owners also make sure that their dog does not infringe upon the rights of others by letting him run loose. Remember, not everyone likes dogs as much as you do and some people are afraid of dogs. Dog parks and dog beaches can be great places for you

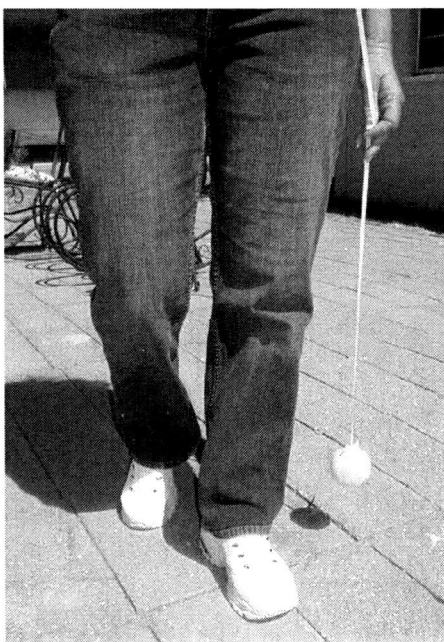

To get an idea of what your dog feels at the end of a leash, try walking with a tennis ball tied to a string. Watch what happens to the ball if you move your arms too much, turn too quickly, or don't walk smoothly and in a straight line.

to exercise your dog off leash but, if your dog is aggressive toward other dogs, then do not take him to an off leash dog park or beach. Many dog parks have separate areas for small dogs and puppies. If your local dog park does not, be very careful about letting your puppy play off leash with older dogs, or letting your small dog loose with unknown large dogs.

— Chapter 10 —

Calling All Dogs

"Boomer, come. ... Boomer?! ... Boomer! Come! ... Boomer!! ... BOOMER! COME!! ... #*&#%*, BOOMER!! GET OVER HERE!!! ... BOOMER!! BOOMER!! ... *%#$ &*#." Does this sound familiar?

Everybody wants a dog that will reliably come when called, but it is one of the hardest things for pet owners to teach. Owners are often is a hurry to teach this, but it takes time and patience to train. Try to imagine being a dog and having just discovered a most intriguing and beckoning smell across the street. Tearing yourself away from it to see what that boring human you live with wants takes a tremendous amount of willpower! You have to teach your dog that there will always be a very good reason for him to come to you. If you are calling your dog for punishment, you will likely fail. NEVER CALL YOUR

DOG TO DISCIPLINE HIM. If you call him for punishment, your dog will learn that it's better NOT to come when called.

In the sport of Obedience, dogs are required to come when called and sit in front of and facing the owner. This is called a recall. The command for the recall is "come". When commanded to "finish," the dog must quickly go to the owner's left side and sit facing forward at the owner's left foot, the dog's shoulder in line with the owner's left hip. This chapter is not about teaching a formal recall. It is about teaching your dog that whenever you call him, something very good happens to him. Your pet dog does not have to sprint to you and sit squarely in front of you when you call. Training a dog to come is only about getting your pet to come to you every time you call. He can sit behind you or leap into your arms if he wants. However, it is a good idea to teach your dog to sit or stand within reach so you can take hold of his collar, or put a leash on him if necessary. Of course, you can train a formal recall if you want. The principles are the same.

There are really only two basic things that are important to dogs and the most valuable thing is food (never mind about the other thing). Always use a very tasty food reward to teach your dog to come when called. Most dogs love bits of hot dog or chicken.

Decide on one unique word or sound that you will use for the rest of your dog's life when you absolutely need him to come to you immediately. Many people use the word "come". It really doesn't matter what the word is. I once read an article about a dog who came when his owner called "free beer!" The Special Signal does not have to be a word. You might want to incorporate a unique, but not too complicated whistle. Most dogs respond well to a whistle. Whistles are not as prone to emotional interpretation as a spoken word. If you can whistle, I recommend you try it. If you are not good at whistling, remember that in a real emergency, you will probably be even worse! Stick with a verbal signal if you are not a good whistler.

Teaching a puppy to come to you is easy. A puppy is usually happy to come to you and follow you around. You may not need a leash on your puppy for this exercise if you are training him indoors. If you are training an adult dog, use a leash. You do need to have your dog in a small enough area that you can control his movement. A hallway is a great place to teach. It is a built-in tunnel back to your arms. Be sure you have treats with you before you start.

Squat down and with your happiest, most excited voice, call your dog using your Special Signal. Clap your hands, snap your fingers, repeat the word, run backwards, call your dog's name and use your body language to invite him to play. Do whatever you need to do to convince him you are very interesting and worth investigating. When he does come to you (and he will) give him a treat and love, pet and praise him. Act as if you have not seen him in ages! This is the routine every time you use the Special Signal. Always reward with a treat or do not use the Special Signal. Never let him refuse to come to you when you use the Special Signal. Remember to always reward the correct response to the Special Signal with a favorite treat. The only time you do not reward with a treat for coming with the Special Signal is in a real emergency when you may not have a treat in your pocket.

When your dog is reliable about coming to you in the hall, train him in a different area of the house. When he is reliable there, take him outside on a leash and teach him to come to you in a place where there are distractions. When practicing "off leash" in new situations or with strong distractions, it is helpful to use a long (30- to 50-foot) leash. Be patient and be interesting to your dog. If you think your dog has mastered the recall on leash, start to practice off leash in the house and in a fenced area. Continue to challenge your dog's mind with new situations but set him up to win, not to fail. Remember it takes many months to develop a good recall so don't give up. Be patient at each step and don't try to progress to the next step too quickly.

Some examples of when to use the Special Signal are: when calling your dog for dinner or for a treat; when calling him to play his favorite game; if your dog is in danger; or if your dog is acting inappropriately toward other animals or people. Never use the Special Signal for something the dog considers unpleasant. If you use the word to call your dog to stop him from playing, from hunting or from sniffing interesting smells, or to bathe or discipline her, the word is ruined. If you use the word needlessly, or use the word without having a way to ensure that she will come to to you, the word is ruined because the dog will learn that it has no real meaning for her. If you have used the word in any of the situations mentioned above, then you should find a new word or sound and start the training over with the new word.

Use a different word or phrase such as "Let's go!" to teach your dog it is time to stop playing and come in the house, leave the dog park, take a bath, and other less than pleasant things for dogs. Teach "Let's go!" by rewarding with treats and praise and encouragement as you would the Special Signal. However, do not use the command out of context. The differences in the two commands are when you use them and how you reward for them. When your dog has learned what you want him to do, you can reward the "Let's go!" with just praise and an occasional treat. Eventually, you will only need to reward with praise.

— Chapter 11 —

Using Commands and Concepts in Real Life

Dog owners have a hard time correlating the commands they teach their dogs to everyday situations. I know some people who diligently taught their dog the "leave it" command but when the dog is tempted to pick up some stinky thing off the ground during a walk, it never occurs to them to tell their dog to "leave it." Instead, they use other words, usually, "Don't eat that!" "Hey!" "No!" "(Dog's Name!)" "Here!" or "Yuk!" Through training and practice, the dog has learned that "leave it" means to leave something alone, but the owner has not learned. One of the hardest parts of dog training is training yourself! After training your dog to understand a few commands, it is a shame to use them only when you are in a formal training environment. The reason for teaching your dog commands is to have a way to control his behavior. When your dog learns "leave it", use that command to tell him to leave a piece of dog food, leave a stinky thing on the ground, leave the cat, leave a sock, or leave another dog alone. Think before you react to your dog. The ability to use a concept anywhere it is appropriate is called generalization. Dogs also have difficulty generalizing and it is important to practice every command in a variety

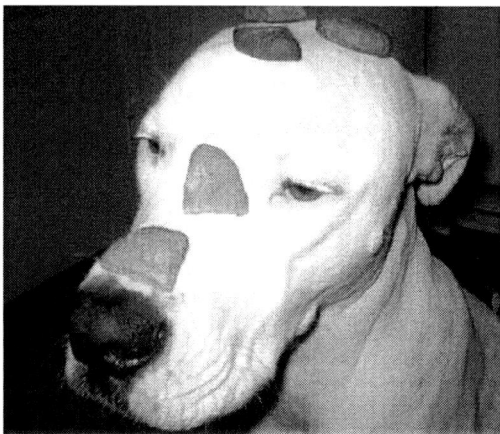

Cooper shows off his "leave it" skills. Those are dog biscuits on his head. "Leave it" is easy for Cooper. His owner Karen taught him to balance many things on his head including loaves of bread, shoes, bottles, fruit, rolls of toilet paper, coffee pots, and short stacks of folded laundry.

of places. Dogs who are trained to "sit" only while the owner watches TV don't understand that they can "sit" on command if the owner is standing, in a room with no TV, or outdoors. Owners who practice the "leave it" command only in a set-up situation do not think to use it in a real life situation.

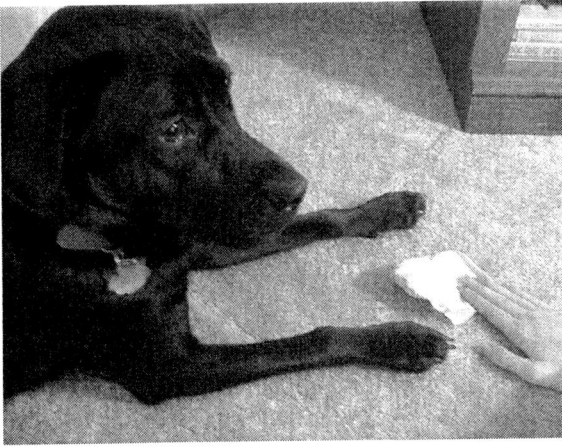

Anastacia teaches Wesley to "leave it". One move from him and her hand covers the tissue as she says "Eh! Leave it!" When Wesley stops going for the tissue, she will immediately reward him with a tasty treat.

— Chapter 12 —

Some Simple Solutions to Common Problems

What humans consider problem behaviors are usually just normal dog behaviors. Normal dogs chew, bark, dig and enjoy eating and rolling in stinky stuff. It is up to us to teach them when those behaviors are inappropriate. Dogs need to chew, so we need to provide them with something acceptable to chew. If your dog chews on the chair leg, interrupt him by clapping your hands and saying "Hey!" When he stops, tell him he is a good dog and hand him something appropriate to chew (a bone or chew toy). When he takes the chew, tell him he is a good dog. Repeat as necessary.

Owners often give their puppies an old sock to play tug-o-war or an old shoe to use as a chew toy. It is hard for dogs to understand the difference between that particular item of clothing and any other item of clothing. To prevent your dog from getting into the laundry basket or clothes closet and chewing your personal items, do not encourage the behavior by giving the dog personal items as toys.

Get and keep your dog's attention. Learning does not happen unless your dog is paying attention to you. Be the most interesting thing in your dog's environment. Start with your dog's name (so he knows you are talking to him) then say, "look." When he looks at you, reward him. Begin to reward him any time he looks at you and he will look at you more. Then, ask him to "look" when you need him to pay attention to you instead of another dog, person or other distraction.

Dog proof your home. If your dog chews your clothes, shoes and other personal items, you must keep them out of reach. Keep clothes and shoes picked up and off the floor. Close doors or use a baby gate to keep the dog out of an area. Use wastebaskets with lids and empty them daily to prevent the dog from being tempted by the smell. Some dogs love to take the end of a roll of toilet paper and run through the house with it. If you have one of those dogs, hang the roll so the end pulls out from the top instead the bottom of the roll.

Contain your dog. If your dog is not housetrained or if he chews furniture or other inappropriate objects, do not give him free run of the house until he is fully trained. If you cannot supervise him, put him in a dog crate or a portable kennel. Crate training is discussed further in Chapter 7. Most dogs do not mind being in a kennel for a few hours and just sleep while you are gone. Puppies should not be crated for more than a couple of hours, and an adult dog no more six, without having an opportunity to relieve themselves and walk around a little. Go home from work during lunch breaks or have a friend look in on him for you, or leave him at a doggie daycare. Many municipalities have ordinances against keeping a dog tied up or left loose outside in the yard while the owner is away. Be sure you know what the laws are in your area.

Exercise your dog. Boredom is the cause of many behavior problems. A bored dog might chew, dig, jump fences or bark incessantly. Most urban dogs are under-exercised. You will know if your dog has had enough exercise if afterward he is lying by your side, happily chewing a bone or chew toy. A tired dog is a well-behaved dog.

Be patient. Some commands, such as "come" and "stay" can take almost a year of practice before your dog will obey them reliably in all situations. A common mistake in training is trying to progress too quickly. A dog learns at his own pace. When teaching "stay", the first few "stays" are only two or three seconds long, with the dog on a leash next to you. When he can "stay" for that length of time, gradually add more seconds. If your dog breaks the "stay", you have progressed too quickly. Train a little longer at the number of seconds that your dog can "stay". Gradually add more distance between you and your dog. If your dog breaks the "stay", again, you have tried to progress too quickly. Go back to the distance where the dog can "stay" and train there a little longer. Either increase duration or increase distance, but do not increase them both at the same time.

Visit your veterinarian regularly. A healthy dog is a happy dog. Your dog should get regular check-ups and be vaccinated on schedule. If your dog's behavior changes suddenly, see your veterinarian. It could be a symptom of illness. Relapses in housetraining can be a sign of a bacterial or viral infection. Mood changes can be a symptom of serious illness.

— Chapter 13 —

Seeking a Professional Trainer

Most people do not hesitate to consult a professional for things in which they are not an expert, and yet some people think nothing of trying to train their dogs without help. If you need help, or would just like to train with a group of other dog owners, look in the telephone book for a dog club or private trainer in your area. Before you commit to a class, compare the cost of joining a club with the cost of group classes provided by a private trainer. Professional trainers' organizations have online member directories you can search. Ask your veterinarian, groomer, and other dog owners for referrals. Many people say they can train a dog or cure a behavior problem whether they can or not. The person you choose to help you should be an experienced, courteous, ethical professional who can provide good references. Good trainers have credentials. They like people and dogs and enjoy working with both. They may prefer not to work with a particular breed, but they do not discriminate against certain breeds, calling them aggressive, stubborn, or not trainable. They may or may not be flexible when it comes to the use of certain types of training equipment, but they are happy to explain why they have a preference. Good trainers know the different personality types of dogs and people and can tailor their training and instruction techniques accordingly. Don't just take somebody's word about what is best for your dog. If you do not feel comfortable with a trainer's methods, find another trainer.

Statistically, people who own pets are healthier and happier than those who do not. Raising your dog should not raise your blood pressure! If you are frustrated or unhappy about training your dog, talk to a trainer. The joys of owning a well-trained dog far outweigh the time and money you invest in training.

— About the Author —

Kathie Compton is a **Certified Dog Behavior Consultant** and **Certified Pet Dog Trainer**, independently certified by the *Certification Council for Pet Dog Trainers* (CCPDT.org) and the *International Association of Animal Behavior Consultants* (IAABC.org). She is a full member of the *Association of Pet Dog Trainers* (APDT.com), a professional member of the *Animal Behavior Management Alliance*, and is is an *American Kennel Club (AKC) Approved Evaluator* for the "Canine Good Citizen" program. Locally, she is a member of the *Responsible Pet Owners Association* (RPOA.org) and the *Jeff Davis County Humane Society*. As a volunteer, Kathie is an actively involved member of IAABC, provides behavior assessments for city animal control and shelter services, is project leader/trainer for the Presidio County 4-H dog club, and conducts Bite Prevention and other presentations for educational seminars and workshops. In addition to **Dogs... *Made Easy!*** *A New Owner's Manual*, she has written educational articles for newspapers, websites, and internet forums. Kathie is the owner of mARFa Dog Training in Marfa, Texas.